D0590320

GREAT RAILWAY PHOTOGRAPHERs

HENRY PRIESTLEY

Presented by Colin Garratt

in association with Henry Priestley

PUBLISHER'S APPEAL

Henry Priestley's legacy of railway negatives was sold piecemeal during the mid-1990s unlike his British tramway pictures which are held exclusively by the National Tramway Museum at Crich. It is Milepost's remit to put together a representative selection of Henry Priestley's railway work in one co-ordinated library. This endeavour has Henry Priestley's support and cooperation. Widespread assistance from individuals nationwide has already allowed considerable progress to be made.
We therefore appeal to anyone who has purchased Priestley negatives or knows where any are located to contact Milepost with a view to a few being transferred to the Priestley archive, either in the form of donations, purchases or exchange for other negatives. The totality of Henry Priestley's railway work constitutes a national heirloom and Milepost consider it vital to conserve in digital form a representative selection covering all areas of his endeavour in one permanent collection.

Milepost wish to thank Leicestershire Record Office and Nottinghamshire Local Studies Library for making available their Priestley negatives for the production of this book. Their assistance enabled a number of important pictures to be included.

Copyright ©1996 text and design Milepost 92$\frac{1}{2}$

This edition first published in 1996 by Milepost Publishing in association with
Arcturus Publishing Limited

for

Selectabook
Folly Road, Roundway, Devizes, Wilts. SN10 2HR

Milepost Publishing is a division of Milepost 92$\frac{1}{2}$
Colin Garratt's audio-visual/video production,
photographic service and picture library for the railway industry.
Milepost also conserves and markets historic collections of negatives and transparencies

Designed by Milepost and Just My Type.

Printed and bound in Great Britain

ISBN 1 900193 50 7

All rights reserved. No part of this book may be reproduced, or transmitted
in any form or by any means, electronic or mechanical,
including photocopying, recording or by any information storage or retrieval system,
without the prior permission, in writing, of the copyright holders.

Milepost 92$\frac{1}{2}$
Newton Harcourt
Leicestershire
LE8 9FH
Tel 0116 2592068

MILEPOST

PREVIOUS PAGE : Ground frame in Mileage Yard, Gloucester.

INTRODUCTION
by Colin Garratt

There are moments when I regard Henry Priestley as the finest railway photographer of all time. Obviously one should be very careful in making so wide a generalisation and yet looking at his pictures is like reading a great novel; the content, the logic and the interrelationship of the story - in this case the expression given to the legend of our railway history. You bask in the elegance of the pictorial composition before sensing the intellect which lies behind the picture's conception. You perceive a vigorous photographic awareness which locks like a magnet on to any exciting event which, in the micro-second of time happens to present itself. One is then ready to scan the picture again; this time to see a broader and more fulfilling perspective. I know of no other photographer who conjures such a complete expression of the way our railways were.

Almost all the content of the original negatives has been printed although I have made small adaptations. The prints were created by Ian Brown L.R.P.S. and the originals from which this

BELOW : *Hampton Loade on the 22nd August 1961, long before the preservation of the Severn Valley Railway was thought of. The 2.05 Kidderminster to Salop train stands in the station in the form of one of the Great Western Railway's diesel railcars of the 1930s - the precursors of today's D.M.U.s. Though primarily for branch line and cross country service these units fulfilled other fascinating tasks, including two sandwiched together, with a restaurant car in between, on Birmingham to Cardiff turns - services which knocked half an hour from the timing of conventional trains.*

book was taken are almost certainly the finest printed manifestations of Henry Priestley's negatives to date.

Ian Brown worked painstakingly to yield every bit of the negative's potential with many prints taking over two hours to make. He tried to recapture the scene as Henry Priestley saw it. The prints are full bodied containing rich blacks and brilliant whites with the widest possible range of mid tones to reveal all the subtleties of detail contained within each negative. Every negative was different, the greatest problem being to find the right balance throughout the picture; most problematic being the sky areas which often required up to six times more exposure than the rest of the negative whilst the locomotives were often at considerable variance to the landscape around them. It was heartening to both Ian and myself that my interpretation of the negatives and the

ABOVE : *An ex-L. &S.W.R. M7 Class 0-4-4T at Bere Alston on 15.8.60 for Plymouth locals. An O2 tank worked the Callington branch.*

quality of his prints both met with the complete satisfaction of Henry Priestley himself.

The history of painting is concerned with artists who have excelled in particular aspects of the visual spectrum; the chiaroscuro of Rembrandt; the draughtsmanship of Canaletto; the stylised countryside and society of Stubbs; the luminosity of The Impressionists; the spatial three dimensionalism of Cezanne, the vivid expressionism of Munch or the stark industrial landscapes of Lowry are random instances which immediately spring to mind. A parallel in railway photographic art would be found in Ivo Peter's magnificent evocations of the Somerset and Dorset; Eric Treacy's vivid and nostalgic glorification of steam's Indian Summer; Maurice Earley's artistic and technical perfection of front three quarter views of Great Western trains; H.C.Casserley's endearing factual account of the diversity of designs, through to the harrowing run down of the steam age, amid the rapidly declining infrastructure of the Industrial Revolution, as portrayed by Colin Gifford.

Priestley's work contains elements of all of these photographs; rather like Turner, often regarded as Britain's greatest painter, who combinined draughtsmanship, light, historical allusion, legend and fantasy in an incomparable coming together of all disciplines.

I grieve for the lack of railway infrastructure in the work of many famous names. Not so much as a station appears, not so much as a factory or even a person, notwithstanding that railways were once the heartbeat of society, industry and commerce. In truth, the steam train was but one element in the fabulous world of railways; it was a world unto itself with its own disciplines and traditions; a world bedecked in civil and engineering triumphs. The spell cast by the railway was overwhelming and although the steam train animated and invigorated that environment it was surely but the principal actor on a stage, not the be all and end all of the whole production.

In following the wider topographical approach, as Henry Priestley has done throughout his long photographic career, it must follow that his trains do not have the same intensity of presence as in a classic Earley or Treacy, indeed many of the best Priestleys don't contain a train at all whilst

ABOVE : *Former G.W.R. Castle Class No. 5076 "Gladiator" approaches the flat crossing at Dunball on the former Bristol and Exeter Railway.*

others, equally compellingly, show modern trains - often humble DMUs.

And there is another essential distinction to be made. Many of the great names in railway photography tend to concentrate on main lines and the most flamboyant expresses with individuals haunting the same well known areas of trackside over several generations. Henry Priestley's aim, from the 1920s, was to record every station and junction, embracing its unique topography, its ambience and

ABOVE : *The view northwards from Loughborough Station showing the Brush works on the right, complete with the famous falcon. Opposite is the fine goods yard which served this once important industrial town.*

distinctive style of infrastructure - most of which dated back to the various practices of the pre-grouping companies.

Future historians will look to Priestley with increasing interest. Our steam trains are still with us; we have, and surely always will have, Flying Scotsman, Mallard, Royal Scot, Castles, Kings and Merchant Navys, but the legend of the railway, with all its incredible diversity, has been ripped from the face of the earth and its documentation in so elegant and informative a way will become an essential historical document.

Henry Priestley was not just a photographer of railways; he has an incomparable legacy of tramway pictures and was a prolific photographer of churches too. His British tramway pictures have fortunately passed to the National Tramway Museum at Crich and the authorities there will readily agree that his is the finest pictorial legacy of the tramway age ever recorded. The church and architectural pictures passed to the National Archive Museum but tragically his railway legacy of some 12,000 negatives - which I can only say constituted a national heirloom - was sold off piecemeal during the early 1990s.

Henry Priestley holds many other distinctions. His active railway photography has spanned an amazing 71 years and he continues to take pictures today and is probably the oldest regularly practising railway photographer in Britain. Henry Benjamin Priestley was born in the reign of King Edward VII at South Ossett in the West Riding. He taught chemistry and physics before gaining an MA from London University. He was headmaster of a Grammar School, from 1950 until 1975.

His first recollection of a train was on a journey from Cardiff to Gloucester, when a de-railment caused his train to be stopped just short of its destination. He remembers being lifted down on to the ballast - an enormous drop - and recalls following a footpath into the city. On the way he passed a tram which appeared to be discharging water into the Severn. He later found out it was drawing water from the river for laying dust on the city streets.

Henry Priestley's first railway photograph was taken in 1925. It depicted the Rhymney Railway Station in Cardiff before it was bulldozed, after which that company's trains used platforms at the Taff Vale station. Featured was a former Rhymney 0-6-2T. So from the very beginning a topographical approach was apparent - that first picture being taken because the station was about to be demolished. His first tramway picture, taken in City Road Cardiff, is dated 1927 and this also records a scene which was about to be radically altered.

His approach to photography was influenced by T.R.Perkins, who wrote in the early editions of The Railway Magazine. Perkins's aim was to travel on every railway in Britain, a formidable undertaking in the 1920s, and especially so for a practising chemist with a shop in Henley in Arden; as Henry has pointed out, his free time would only have been on Saturday afternoons, Sundays and a two week annual holiday. The young Priestley sought every T.R.Perkins column he could find and emulated Perkin's task - but with a camera!

ABOVE : *Ollerton was on the former Lancashire Derbyshire and East Coast Railway which was incorporated into the Great Central. This scene, taken on 4.12.54 depicts, Robinson Class C13 4-4-2T No. 67437.*

During my interviews with Henry Priestley he emphasised, to my enormous surprise, that his photography was subjective; done for his own personal collection. He was not consciously working for posterity and in the early years at least, knew of no other individuals doing similar work. When he met W.A.Camwell in later years he was grateful to find a kindred spirit. This did not mean that Priestley lacked commitment; on the contrary, he was running a race against time, often dashing off at short notice to cover some threatened line that he had heard about at the last minute.

One of the most engaging aspects of the legacy is the widespread inclusion of Henry's two sons in his pictures. They were not dragooned into appearing; they willingly went on many of his trips. Rather than their appearance being for artistic reasons in the composition. Henry states that they were placed there "so that he could keep his eye on them"! and yet they add an incomparable element to many scenes, being woven into the compositions providing balance, animation and perspective. Henry Priestley's photography is self taught; he has learnt "on the job". Many pictures have been done by trial and error and "duds" have been remade wherever possible - often years after the original was taken. One of his most successful trips was a week spent at Duns in Berwickshire, during which he recorded steam trains in most stations on the East Coast Main Line between Newcastle and Edinburgh and on the Waverley Line between Edinburgh and Carlisle.

ABOVE : *Ordsall Crossing, Retford with an original Robinson Class 04, 2-8-0. Behind the camera was the G.N./G.C. Flat Crossing.*

I must conclude that meeting and working with Henry Priestley has been a privilege. His knowledge, enthusiasm and vigour have been an inspiration to all of us at Milepost as we strive to put together again as much of his pictorial legacy as possible in order to hand on to posterity a properly co-ordinated and conserved Priestley library. My meetings and interviews with Henry always concluded with a delightful trip to a nearby cafe for tea and muffins and these occasions, along with the appreciation of his art, have become treasured memories which will remain with me for the rest of my days.

Colin Garratt,
Milepost 92^1/$_2$,
Newton Harcourt,
Leicestershire,
August 1996

ABOVE : *Lostock Gralam, on the former Cheshire Lines Committee's railway, with an L.N.E.R. Class 02, 2-8-0 in a beautifully balanced composition which eloquently features the presence of the Head Shunt to the adjacent goods yard.*

BELOW : *A similar approach is taken in this scene of Nafferton, between Hull and Bridlington.This time with a wagon in the process of being loaded or un-loaded in the goods yard recalling the days when the railways served villages and towns alike without the need for widespread development of the road systems and the environmental contortions and economic inefficiencies they have brought about. H.B.P. pointed out that this location is particularly interesting in that the station house is at right angles to the railway.*

ABOVE : *This vigorous scene at Chesham was taken on the 18th September 1948, with a former Robinson Great Central Class C13, 4-4-2T introduced in 1903. This station was a Metropolitan terminus and the C13 is operating the shuttle up to the main line at Chalfont and Latimer. This is classic Priestley; the essential contours of the C13 have been beautifully caught expressively flanked by the water tower on the left and the fine Metropolitan signal box on the right, along with a fine array of contemporary advertising hoardings. Animation is added by the bustling passengers on the platform and an interesting aside is the new concrete container on the far right which contained grit for the platform surfaces in icy weather.*

ABOVE : *On the 24th March 1962 the 2.25 Saturdays only train from Mansfield to Worksop pauses at Langwith behind former L.M.S. Fairburn 2-6-4T No. 42222. The bustling engine impatiently blowing off contrasts well with the ladies, purposefully setting off for home after a shopping trip. This line was worked by former Midland Railway 0-4-4Ts for many years until the displaced Tilbury 4-4-2Ts, with all their inadequacies, took over as Cinderella Traction. H.B.P. points out that, by the 1960s, ladies were freely using railways, contrasting with the limitations of former years, when ladies travelled in fear of molestation. The shadow of the station lamp and nameboard and the adjacent fencing add further topographical detail making excellent use of an otherwise featureless platform area.*

LEFT, Below : *Prudhoe Ovingham was one of many stations on the former North Eastern Railway's Newcastle to Carlisle line. The train is headed by ex N.E.R Class G5, 7316 allocated to 52C depot and the train, the 1.10PM from Hexham to North Wylam. The G5s consisted of a class of 110 engines built by the North Eastern between 1894 and 1901. H.B.P. recalls that Prudhoe was the location of a characteristic station house. Again bustle and urgency are predominant; the engine blows off impatiently, the semaphore is lowered clear for departure these elements are heightened by the lady dashing out of the booking hall on to the platform.*

ABOVE : *Kirkby Station junction, on the former Midland Railway in a stirring scene taken on an Agfa Silette camera, which gave pin sharp negatives and which, in its final modified form, was the finest camera H.B.P. had. The former L.M.S. 4F, 0-6-0 is pilot to a Stanier Class 8, 2-8-0 in a well balanced composition framed by the distant footbridge and accentuated by the debris in the left foreground.*

RIGHT, Below : *A scene at Worksop looking east towards Retford on the 22nd August 1964 featuring Austerity 2-8-0, No. 90504 allocated to 36E, caught clanking through the station with a coal train. The magnificent overbridge framing the scene is graced by H.B.P.'s two boys, just visible through the girderwork. The siding on the extreme right is where the Midland services from Nottingham were stabled and a three coach train can be seen waiting to move back into the station for the return journey.*

ABOVE : *The movement of another double headed freight is revealed in this scene of an L.M.S. 4F, 0-6-0 piloting a former wartime Austerity 2-8-0 through Plumtree on the Midland Main Line southwards from Nottingham to Melton. The date is 5th November 1956 and the station had already closed to passengers. In addition to H.B.P's two sons, busily spotting at the "platform end", on-lookers have stopped to watch from the road bridge what must have been, by any standards, a rousing audio-visual spectacular. The station house is typical of the stately designs on this alternative Midland Railway route from London to the North.*

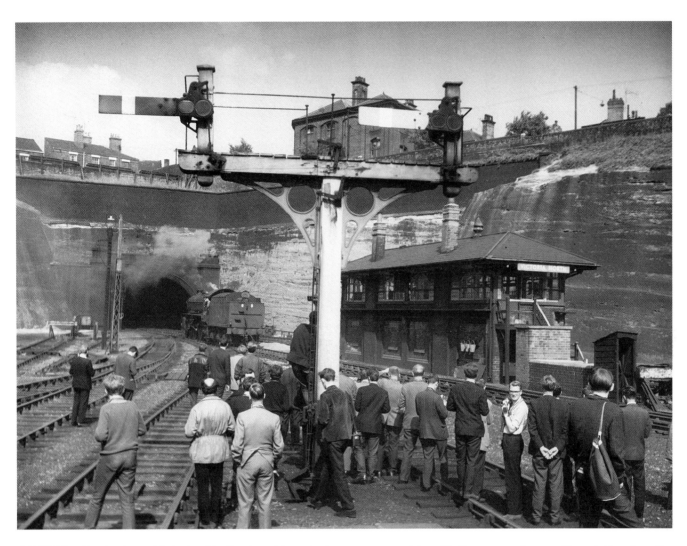

ABOVE : *Nottingham Victoria, North signal box juxtaposes superbly with the semaphores. The station has the aura of being condemned, its latter day glory being the three semi-fasts per day along the former Great Central Main Line to London Marylebone.*

LEFT, above : *H.B.P. enjoyed Railtours and this Stephenson Locomotive Society outing was headed by Midland Railway designed Simple 4-4-0 No. 40646. The tour was on the 14th April 1962 and visited such places as Northampton, Oxford and Verny Junction - the picture here being taken during a stop at Weedon. H.B.P. was introduced to this tour by W.A. Camwell, a keen participant in the S.L.S. The figures in this and the adjacent pictures show the smartness of dress some 40 years ago, revealing how, by stealth, we have become a far more casually dressed society. The foreground shadows again provide additional and relevant information and augment the mass of people. Priestley uses these to make a vigorous contrast with the individuals themselves.*

LEFT, below : *Another notable day out was the Locomotive Club of Great Britain's Great Central Rail tour which featured a double headed B1 seen here at Nottingham, Victoria. This huge area is now the site of the Nottingham Victoria shopping centre.*

ABOVE : *H.B.P. refers to the Great Central shed at Retford as Thrumpton. The Great Northern and Great Central depots were considered one depot although they were almost half a mile apart. The Great Central shed was closed in January 1965 and demolished to make way for the construction of the Retford dive-under. This study, taken alongside the belt operated coaling stage, depicts one of the lovely ex- North Eastern Railway's 3 cylinder B16, 4-6-0s.*

RIGHT, above : *Retford Great Northern shed with a pair of stored Gresley 02, 2-8-0s. These were Gresley's first three cylinder locomotives appearing in 1918. H.B.P. stated that they were not particularly successful and once diesels began to appear were quickly put into store often with bags on their chimneys. One of the popular Robinson 04, 2-8-0s of 1911 passes with a Trip Freight.*

RIGHT, centre : *Retford Great Northern shed on the 18th August 1959. The scene characteristically shows small boys racing across the shed yard in those heady pre-electronic media days when the greatest fascination for children was to be found either on the railway or the football pitch - or for many boys, both.*

RIGHT, below : *Another view of Thrumpton Great Central depot in Retford, taken on 26th June 1959 and showing one of Robinson's former Great Central Pom-Pom J11. 0-6-0s under the sheer legs. The J11s were so named on account of the explosive exhaust beats resembling the Pom-Pom guns of World War 1. H.B.P. made the point that his best picture of a locomotive under the sheer legs was of an M7 at Fratton.*

ABOVE : *Thompson B1 Class 4-6-0 No. 61088 approaches Kirkby Laythorpe on the 27th July 1963 with the 2.11 Mablethorpe to Leicester Great Central special. On the ordnance survey map this location is "Frenchified" being known as Kirkby la Thorpe. The children here are not H.B.P.'s; he recalls that they were going in and out of the signal box and were, presumably, the signalman's son and daughter.*

LEFT, above : *The sylvan setting of Branston and Heighington station, which was the first south of Lincoln on the Great Northern, Great Eastern joint line to Sleaford. H.B.P.'s two sons are seen in animated posture eager to identify K3 Class 61807, a Lincoln engine, in this scene taken on the 19th May 1957.*

LEFT, below : *A similar eagerness is portrayed here by H.B.P.'s two sons as they identify former Great Central Director 62670 "Marne" as it approaches Burton Joyce with the 5.05 Lincoln to Derby train on the 1st September 1956. This service was regularly worked by Great Central Directors allocated to Lincoln depot. The Midland Railway's 5 mile post on the right measures the distance from Nottingham.*

ABOVE : *This is another of H.B.P.'s favourite pictures and one whose atmosphere depends entirely on a grey, wet day. H.B.P. emphasised that "the cloud of smoke and steam would not be so visible had the weather been better". Taken on 16th June 1956, the scene depicts Gresley V2 Class 60817 bursting through Staveley Central Station on the Great Central Main Line. One of H.B.P.'s boys makes a gallant pose in the left foreground eager to identify the emerging V2.*

ABOVE : *Trowell on the Midland Railway's direct line to Sheffield from Trent saw extensive coal traffic via Toton epitomised by the two approaching trains photographed on the 13th April 1957 and headed by Stanier 8F, 2-8-0s, the leading one on the up fast. Upwards of sixty 8Fs were allocated to Toton during the 1950s. There can be few better ways of featuring semaphore signals and integrating them into the railway environment than the example depicted here.*

ABOVE : *Chesterfield Midland, overshadowed by the crooked spire, makes a magnificent railway setting for an L.M.S. 4F, 0-6-0. Note the positioning of H.B.P.'s two boys in relation to the approaching train and also the platform mounted semaphore.*

ABOVE : *Another of H.B.P.'s favourite pictures is this scene at Mansfield taken during Christmastide in 1953. Originally H.B.P. thought that it might have been taken on Christmas day but reference to the negative sourced the date as 29th December. H.B.P. lived nearby and took the opportunity of going to the station to record this scene in arctic conditions when, despite the brazier, the water column was frozen. Stanier 2-6-2T No. 40175 is seen at the head of a train from Worksop to Nottingham.*

ABOVE : *Handforth Station on a pouring wet day in August 1962. At the platform a Class 304 E.M.U. stands with the 3.35 Manchester Oxford Road to Crewe as West Coast Electric E3025 speeds by at the head of the 1.44 Birmingham to Manchester. This picture is a perfect example of H.D.P. catching the instant and transforming an otherwise routine scene into an exciting occurrence which conveys all the urgency and thrill of the railway despite the impending passing of steam.*

RIGHT : *A study in the same mould as the picture opposite and a composition graphically depicting the train, the Midland Railway signal box, cantilevered over the platform and the solitary workman - having descended from the train - purposefully climbs the wooden steps, homebound. With the expressive contrasts of a Munch painting a small boy sits alone on the platform eagerly awaiting more exciting events than the passing D.M.U. on a Leicester to Nottingham service.*

PREVIOUS PAGES, left, above : *This rare scene was taken on the remoteness of the Midland Railway's Barnoldswick branch which ended in sidings after the station level crossing. Taken on the 18th February 1955, the scene depicts Ivatt 2-6-2T No. 41327 with the 3.50 Auto Train to Earby. The two arm signal was possibly the only one left in Britain at that time.*

PREVIOUS PAGES, left, centre and below : *Kirkby Bentinck was the nearest station to Mansfield on the Great Central Main Line. Again, being close to home, H.B.P. took the opportunity of a liberal fall of snow to record these remarkable scenes. The middle picture depicts Austerity 2-8-0, 90410, a Mexborough engine, heading a train of down mineral empties. The figure on the "up" platform is something of a mystery as he is seen again in the lower picture running at full speed chasing Sheffield Darnall B1 No. 61041. Both pictures were made on the 26th February 1955.*

PREVIOUS PAGES, right, above and below : *This evocation shows a Black 5 taken from the Ilkley platform at Skipton. The bitter winter coldness associated with this part of Britain is eloquently portrayed as are the rigours of steam locomotive operations. The scene below is a further witness to the bleak, coldness of Skipton in mid-winter.*

LEFT : *Hope Station in Derbyshire in immaculate guise complete with L.M.S. "Target" station sign.*

LEFT : *The finials on the station board indicate the location of this picture to be the Scottish Highlands, possibly Brodie, West of Forres. Taken on the 28th August 1961, the beauty of this tranquil station scene is much enhanced by the tablet apparatus located proud of the platform end.*

LEFT : *Whatstandwell Station on the Midland Railway's Main Line between Derby and Manchester looking north towards Matlock. A scene dated 22nd February 1957*

ABOVE : *Cromford Station, a little to the north of Whatstandwell, complete with Station Master's pagoda shaped house on the hill. The date of this scene is 20th October 1956.*

BELOW : *Bingham, looking westwards towards Nottingham, on an east-west running section of the former Great Northern Line to Grantham. When the sky was decked in particularly heavy cumulus clouds, H.B.P. avoided the use of a filter as, on occasions, the clouds became more important than the railway. This high summer scene was taken on the 8th July 1955. The Great Northern shunting signal is visibly interlocked with the points.*

ABOVE : H.B.P.'s mastery of capturing the living instant in a micro second of time is epitomised in the movement inherent in this scene of a Stanier 2-6-4T at Kirkby Station junction on a Nottingham to Mansfield service. Cyclists strain at the crossing gates, impatiently waiting for the train to pass; a bustling shopper crosses the bridge; the swirling steam beneath the overbridge indicates a heavy exhaust beat as the train rapidly pulls away. Even the poised semaphore seems anxious to drop back into the "on" position.

ABOVE : *Bustle, excitement and movement are again revealed in this remarkable picture of Long Eaton Station as it was prior to closure and Sawley Junction Station being renamed Long Eaton. The departing train is headed by a former Midland Railway Simple 4-4-0 No. 40585, a Nottingham engine at the head of a Chesterfield to Nottingham service on 23rd February 1959.*

ABOVE : *A K1 Class Mogul 2-6-0 heads a Railtour organised jointly by the Stephenson Locomotive Society and the Manchester Locomotive Society. This tour, which took place on the 31st August 1958, covered many mineral lines and Henry recalls visiting Lanchester, Witton Gilbert, Blackhill and north to the Tyne.*

ABOVE : *H.B.P.'s methodical approach to railway topography is evidenced in these two highly contrasting views of Claypole, on the East Coast Main Line. The first scene looks south as an A1 Pacific approaches. The telegraph pole, which forms a dominant part of the picture's structure, is passing information to the signal box as part of the Great Northern's block telegraph system between Doncaster and Peterborough.*

BELOW : *The lower scene, which looks north towards Newark, was taken some 12 years later.*

ABOVE and BELOW : *Two scenes on the now vanished Cottam Station on the direct Great Central route between Retford and Lincoln - as opposed to the present route via Gainsborough. Near Cottam, the Trent was crossed by a bridge which proved troublesome to maintain and BR were glad to be rid of it when the line closed. In the lower scene, the Ford Zodiac on the right is H.B.P.'s. Both scenes show the instant of token exchange as the signalman has come down from his box. However small and countryfied the location the inevitable produce wagon for pick-up freights was present and forms an intrinsic part of these local scenes*

ABOVE : Langham Junction is on the Midland Railway's main line from Nottingham to London via Melton. In common with Midland Railway practice, this junction is merely a point where the lines open out from two tracks to four. The Midland Railway distribution pole alongside the signal box conveys information from the principal grid into the signal box for block working. The former crossing keeper's house complements the signal box beautifully.

BELOW : Ashwell was on the same route as the above picture and once again a Peak type diesel in the early part of it's working life animates the scene.

ABOVE : *Trent Station was one of the most famous Island Exchange stations in railway history. H.B.P. recalls others such as Broome Junction, Normanton and to some extent, Burton on Trent. In this scene the splendid Midland Railway signal gantry is balanced by the approach of Peak type diesel D1 "Scafell Pike". H.B.P. remembers that he left his two boys in the enclosure for some time whilst the set of pictures were made from the north end of the station. He also recalls that trains for St. Pancras left from either end of Trent station. The Peak is depicted with a southbound goods from Nottingham.*

PREVIOUS PAGES, left, above : *On the 23rd April 1966 a Railtour of Buckinghamshire took place with British Railways Standard 2-6-0 Mogul No. 78036 covering the Great Western and London and North Western lines in the area.*

PREVIOUS PAGES, left, below : *An ex-L. & N.W.R. G2, 0-8-0 on a London and North Western branch line tour seen here between Bescot and Stetchford.*

PREVIOUS PAGES, right, above : *Newark Northgate Station looking north in 1953 with former Manchester Sheffield and Lincolnshire Railway Class N5, 0-6-2T No. 69313 on a branch line Railtour which embraced Bottesford, Long Clawson & Hose and Melton.*

PREVIOUS PAGES, right, centre : *Former Great Northern J52, 0-6-0ST at Hatfield with an outer suburban Railtour on the 14th April 1962.*

PREVIOUS PAGES, right, below : *One of H.B.P.'s most memorable Railtours took place on the 24th August 1952. The occasion was organised jointly by The Stephenson Locomotive Society and The Manchester Locomotive Society to run between Sheffield and Hull and back embracing the Hull and Barnsley main lines. H.B.P. recalls that ex- Midland Railway Belpaire 4-4-0 No. 40726 took the train forward from Sheffield Wicker Station to Cudworth, where former North Eastern Railway D20, 4-4-0 No. 62360 took over. The tour embraced the entire length of the Hull and Barnsley and the few branches it had. Canon Street was the Hull and Barnsley's original terminus in Hull but it was in poor condition and the train ran into Paragon Station instead after which the party visited all three Hull Motive Power Depots. H.B.P. emphasised that the Hull and Barnsley Railway never actually reached Barnsley, finishing at Cudworth Junction in the Midland Railway's five platform station.*

ABOVE : *This picture was made during a tour of the Bristol area behind a Pannier Tank. A variety of Port Lines were visited, along with Canon's Marsh and the Thornbury branch.*

RIGHT, above : *Frome has probably the only surviving country example of a Brunel overall roof. Former Great Western 2251 Class 0-6-0 No. 2213 is seen at the head of the 3.17 train, via Wells, to Yatton on 21st August 1957.*

RIGHT, below : *Brent Knoll, on the Bristol to Exeter line, had a museum hence the reason for H.B.P.s visit on the 9th August 1960. The museum however was closed and he embarked on a photographic session instead producing this scene of Castle Class 4-6-0 No. 4077 "Chepstow Castle". The engine is in uncharacteristically dirty condition but by this time standards were clearly beginning to slip as the end of steam was in sight.*

ABOVE : *Bletchley Station on 14th April 1962 with a Jinty 0-6-0 T acting as station pilot. The flyover in the background was a prime interest in making this picture and was relatively new at the time. H.B.P. described the elegant structure as a white elephant, as it carried the Oxford to Cambridge line, a cross country line which now only operates between Bedford and Bletchley, and Bicester and Oxford, leaving the viaduct virtually unused.*

BELOW : *One of H.B.P.'s "top ten" pictures containing many of the exciting elements he looks for in a photograph; a double headed train, steam and smoke, people in action and the magnificent station board and generic lamps in fine relief. "I had to stop down the aperture to get sufficient depth of field for the station sign and the two locomotives" H.B.P. explained. It is a scene that reveals bustle and movement. H.B.P. was travelling on the train and got out to take this picture which recalls latter day operations on the Great Central. The two locomotives are heading a Nottingham to Marylebone train - one of only three a day during the systematic running down of this, Britain's last main line to London. It is an interesting thought that the Great Central Atlantics of half a century earlier would have reached Marylebone from Nottingham far quicker than the two modern giants.*

ABOVE : *Pinchbeck is located on the Great Eastern and Great Northern joint line between March and Doncaster. It is a superb location with a characteristic awning in silhouette augmented by the oil lamp on the left, along with repeater lamps down the platform. A somersault signal pokes it head over the road bridge, whilst behind the station sign stands a water tower which had presumably nothing to do with the railway. Into this magnificent setting comes the train like an actor on the stage in the form of an up goods headed by Doncaster allocated Gresley 3 cylinder Class 02, 2-8-0 No. 63947. The date is the 30th June 1956.*

BELOW : *The low canopy building of Retford Station on the East Coast Main Line is host to Gresley V2 Class 2-6-2 No. 60850 intently being watched by three boys situated in a dramatically triangular form to the train. The stark oil lamp in the left foreground making a superb balance with the engine in a picture which breathes all the magic of the moment in which it was made.*

ABOVE : *Another St. Pancras scene featuring re-built Royal Scot Class No. 46162 "Queen Victoria's Rifleman". The 14B shedplate indicates that the engine was alocated to Kentish Town and is seen heading the Sunday 11.45 express to Bradford on the 12th March 1961. H.B.P. recalls that size for size, the re-built Scots were the finest engines the L.M.S. had - a view point which was widely held during the 1950s. The re-built Royal Scots came top in the locomotive exchanges of 1948. H.B.P. was also a traveller on this train and he photographed it again at Leicester.*

LEFT, above : *The impending disappearance of Luton North signal box was the reason for this Midland Main Line scene with the B.R. station name board, incorporating Whipsnade Zoo - presumably by changing onto the former Great Northern Line to Dunstable. A later thought is given for Luton Airport and the rail-road airlink.*

LEFT, below : *The hallowed portals of St.Pancras Station provide the backdrop to this magnificent evocation of Nottingham-based Jubilee No. 45620 "North Borneo" preparing to depart with an express for Nottingham on the 2nd April 1956. Again, the immediacy of the moment is completely captured; the blower is on and smoke swirls from the Jubilee's chimney, a passenger has wandered out to have a look at the locomotive before departure whilst the delightful interaction between the locomotive's crew and the guard, was typical of the up-beat feeling in the railway industry during the 1950s. H.B.P. was a passenger on this train.*

ABOVE : H.B.P.'s "top ten" selection rapidly gravitates into a "top hundred" but this one, which remains crystal clear in his memory is definitely one of his pictures of a lifetime. The un-forgettable day was the 10th March 1956 and the crystal clear frosty conditions of early morning in Mansfield inspired him to go to New Basford for photography. The composition is breathtakingly good; the elements sharpened by the oblique lighting and the almost visible movement of the steam and smoke as the 2-8-0 emerges from Carrington Tunnel throwing the raised semaphore into superb relief. This is railway photography at it's very finest, it captures the spell and magical atmosphere of the railway and yet is so rich in detail that it can be read like a page of descriptive text.

ABOVE : *The signalman at Whissendine pensively watches Henry Priestley as he takes this all embracing scene of a Stanier 8F at the head of a rake of down mineral empties on the 11.7.1964.*

LEFT, Below : *One of H.B.P.'s most memorable trips was a stay at Duns in Berwickshire from where he photographed much of the Waverley route and the East Coast Main Line. He recalls that virtually everything from that trip was excellent; he had a good film and was using the Agfa Silette camera, re-built to its final form. Here is one of the scenes from that trip featuring former L.N.E.R. A2 Pacific No. 60516 "Hycilla" caught at Fallodon on the East Coast Main Line with a train of Pullman stock on 7th June 1960.*

ABOVE : *H.B.P. had heard that a Nottingham Crab had been diagrammed to take a Sunday Special to Mablethorpe and made this memorable picture of the train at Mansfield Great Central Station which no longer exists. The sunny Sunday in question was the 2nd August 1959 and the train is composed of two L.M.S. coaches behind the locomotive and the remainder Great Central stock. The train proceeded from Mansfield, over the Great Central line via Clipstone Junction - a section built during World War One.*

ABOVE : *One of the many exiled Tilbury 4-4-2Ts rolls smokely into Elmton and Cresswell Station with a Worksop to Nottingham train via Mansfield. The Tilbury tanks lasted longer on this section than anywhere else off their home ground, and they were almost universally un-popular wherever they went. The train concerned was the 3.40 Worksop to Nottingham and the date is the 19th May 1952. The locomotive was No. 41961 allocated to Mansfield. These engines ran chimney-first away from Nottingham on account of the gradients on this route and the attendant risk of water uncovering the firebox crown.*

BELOW : *A former Great Central Railway Robinson 4-6-2T graces the bay at Aylesbury with a stopping train for Marylebone. The train comprises Metropolitan Suburban stock which provided maximum seating within the minimum coach length.*

LEFT, above, below and ABOVE : *Three views of Sutton in Ashfield Station on the former Great Northern Line from Nottingham to Langwith. Pictures which characterise the very essence of H.B.P.'s ambition to record the topographical diversity of Britain's railway before the mass dismantling of the Beeching years. The fact that today nothing more than a hollow in the ground remains of this location only adds poignancy to the scenes. The B1 with the "soft focus" effect was taken, on the 6th August 1960, through the central window of the station over-bridge, clearly depicted in the picture above left. By this time, H.B.P. recalls, only special passenger trains used this route and both the B1, 4-6-0 and K3 Mogul seen above were likely to have been on Mablethorpe excursions. The K3 is clearly being admired by the lady and her children on the railway footpath above the embankment behind which lines of washing flutter gaily.*

ABOVE : *The dawn of the motor age and the subsequent decline of the railway are epitomised in this reflective scene in North Eastern England. The Wolseley on the left and Ford on the right being balanced respectively by a North Eastern Railway Q6, 0-8-0 and a wartime W.D. Austerity 2-8-0.*

BELOW : *Railway dereliction and the impending motor age are again poignantly revealed here in another study of decay, although the railway's all-pervading superiority is suggested in the crossing priority - the tawdry motorcar with its solitary occupant being subservient to the train.*